FORWARD
by Catherine Bishop

I have only a few thoughts as to what to say in a Forward to this book, but I think these ideas are central to understanding the people and their poetry.

First, I'm not the poet that my mother was and my daughter is. I'm not just being modest; their work outshines any literary efforts I have ever made, and that's all right. Maybe my most important role was to be a genetic conduit between my mother's highly intelligent brain and my daughter's equally brilliant and also marvelously creative brain. I am in awe of both of them and so thankful to have been a part of their lives.

Second, I know that my mother's poetry was often an outpouring of stress, grief, and anxiety. In the midst of a family, she often felt alone and misunderstood, and she poured out these feelings in her sonnets, some of which are heartbreaking. I often wish I had been more attentive to what she was experiencing, but as a young high school and college student with many other things on my mind, I was oblivious to her pain. If there is a positive note, it is that reading Eleanor's poetry has made me more discerning as I interact with other people and try to see into their minds and hearts.

Third, my daughter's poetry strikes me as supremely beautiful at the same time that her words often slice deep into my somewhat complacent view of the world around me. In her tight, forceful lines, Juliet sometimes calls me to examine myself in light of the suffering of other people, and when she writes about joyful experiences, I am transported to stand beside her. It seems impossible that anyone could read her poems and not be touched in some way.

Last, my poetry. Most of my work isn't really "work," as the words and lines seem to put themselves together and pour out onto a page. My poems most often spring from times or experiences that have evoked great joy. They are statements of rejoicing at the beauty and wonder of the natural world, and I hope their tone is a gentle counterpoint to some of the cloudy days we all share from time to time.

Blessings on all who read this book! May your lives reflect the glory of God's creation.

FORWARD
by Juliet Lockwood

When my mother and I set out to put this anthology together, neither of us knew where to begin. My grandmother's copious poetry, so much of it quite lyrical and poignant, felt both a blessing and a burden. How does one sift through and determine, on behalf of someone else no less, what fits, what complements, and what should be left for family only?

On one of my mother's visits to Oregon in 2018, we rented a room at The Arden Forest Inn in Ashland, and spent the morning and early afternoon on their lawn reading through so many of Eleanor's poem, laughing, crying and loving the process. Roughly two years later, a non-fiction book of my mother's came close to conclusion of its completed draft around the same time I was visiting my parents in Kentucky. Whether from the inertia of that project or the odd and immediate frame of mind that the Coronavirus pandemic threw so many people into, we pulled out all the stops in the 10 days I was there and put as many hours as we could manage into making the editorial decisions needed to move forward with this collection.

I treasure much of what I've learned in this process, not only about my mother and grandmother, but about myself. For instance, in looking back at some of the poetry I wrote in my teens and 20s, I realize I used to write with a constant awareness of what I felt was expected of me. While I never shared some of those works with my mother until we started working on this anthology, I realize in some ways, I was still writing for her, or at least writing to reflect what I imagined she would expect of me.

For instance, in "Goddess," the last few lines break from the speaker's previous affect. Careless and caught-up throughout the rest of the poem, the lines, "By morning / I will throb / poisoned and broken," allude to the speaker's expectation of remorse for her wantonness, a remorse I myself never authentically felt. I realize now, at my core, I always knew that my sexuality belonged to me, that it could never be given, taken or cheapened by anything I, or anyone else, could do. Still, I knew instinctually, my mother would disagree on that point, and so I portrayed the speaker in that poem as someone who would regret her actions.

The same can be said, pertaining to what I perceived as societal expectations, in "When I Bleed." While the first 12 lines of the sonnet portray a speaker horrified at the idea of an unwanted pregnancy, the final couplet suggests that she eventually came around the idea and actually hoped to bear a child. In my own pregnancy scares in my teens and 20s, I never experienced even an inkling of such ambivalence. I knew I didn't want a baby to derail my young adult life, no cognitive dissonance in the least. Still, I felt beholden to write as if there were.

Now, in my 40s, I find myself bemused remembering these feelings of obligation. I also realize that I lacked the self-awareness in those days to entirely understand that these portrayals were not intrinsic to me.

By contrast, I cannot think of a better word than intrinsic to describe my affinity for nearly all types of writing. On my Patreon author page, I describe it as, "…something tapping on the inside of my skull, that words, ideas and stories have always demanded I find a way to bring them into the world." I live for the moments I can steal away from everything else and let the inspiration flow. I have far more ideas than I ever have time to write. Still, writing is first and last to me, the one core piece of my soul that, though it has waxed and waned, has never disappeared from my identity.

Another factor that has influenced my identity and my poetry is the importance of place. My poems "Lexington" and "Oregon Blackberry" speak directly to how place has affected my life. While I've not written much poetry about it, another aspect of place in my life that I cannot in good conscience fail to illuminate involves where I live at the time of this publication. While my bio talks about a feeling of coming home when I moved in 2006 to the small-town atmosphere of Grants Pass, Oregon, years later, I would discover a dark undertone to a large portion of the population living in the beautiful region known as the "Rogue Valley."

A despicable past haunts the entire state of Oregon, a past I knew nothing about when I moved here. Racist language in the state's Constitution, finally removed in the early 2000s, established it as a "white-only" state, and "black exclusionary laws" were passed even before that, beginning in 1844 when it was still a territory. In 2020, the entire nation, and indeed the world watched the shameful displays of overt racism in Portland, arguably the most liberal Oregon city.

And where I live in southern Oregon, unfortunately, a significant segment of the population holds even more tightly to racist ideology, both subconsciously, and for some, even quite overtly and unapologetically. My white privilege blinded me to much of it for years after I moved here. I only woke to its depths around 2015, and I have railed against it ever since, mostly through my writing in the form of essays, blogs, and social media posts. In 2020, I also added my presence in person to a few of the local BLM-affiliated marches and demonstrations, but where my body can blend in and get lost in a crowd of demonstrators, my words, my God-given gift, will always stand out, and I intend to use them to the best of my ability to continue in the global march toward social justice. I pray the gift of words passed down through the Lockwood legacy can aid me in that march.

Lockwood is a family name, the maiden name of Eleanor's mother Martha Ann Lockwood Hall. It's my given middle name, and the only portion of my moniker that hasn't changed. I've incorporated it into most all of my online handles and identities. Throughout my life, people have known me as Juliet, Julie, Julia, Jules and even my self-created nickname Bisju, but at the core of my identity, especially my identity as a poet and author, Lockwood remains my anchor and my birthright.

And that holds true for this collection as well. The line of women represented in these pages begins and ends with Lockwood, a legacy of hardiness, a legacy of lyricism, a legacy of spirited resilient women.

TABLE OF CONTENTS

INTRODUCTION

Over three generations stretching back more than a century, the Lockwood women have discovered their poet's heart. The daughter, granddaughter and great granddaughter of Martha Ann Lockwood Hall, each woman came to the practice of poetry in her own way and time. Beginning with Eleanor, born in 1919, and continuing with Catherine (1949), and Juliet (1979), these women turned to the words that came to them in times of joy and times of tribulation. Shaped by history, place, and life experiences, each voice resounds differently, yet their compositions often come together in unplanned and unexpected parallels.

Eleanor wrote sporadically in her youth, but the majority of her work comes from more than 250 sonnets crafted during a difficult stretch of her mid-life. Catherine, on the other hand, most often found her voice through awe-inspiring experiences in nature and in times of celebration and exultation. And Juliet's muse continually prompts her to put pen to paper or fingers to keyboard about anything and everything, from highly emotional topics to the seemingly-mundane. At times, each poet has allowed her creativity to run freely, expressing poignant impressions about experiences both real and imagined.

You're invited to partake of their unique offerings, learn more about each woman as an individual, and muse with them at their distinct voices as well as the sporadic, unintentional and uncanny similarities between poems separated by decades in their composition. This collection represents each generation taking her place in a matrilineal line that passed down a love and a talent for the weaving of words.

We offer it in celebration and gratitude.

I. ON STRIVING

SONNET 42
Eleanor Hayden - 1967

The single-minded search for knowledge may
So close the ear and blind the eye to all
Diverting sound and sight that human need
May go unheeded at the wailing wall.
And on the other hand emotion may
Consume the strength, and leave the hungry mind
Too weak to grasp what knowledge comes its way.
Too much of anything is bad. To find
A balance, that would seem to be the key:
The golden mean — a right relationship —
Will free both mind and heart for fullest growth.
But somehow this will never do for me:
Such limits make of life a deadly trip!
I have to try the limits of them both.

NO LIMITS
Juliet Lockwood – 2005

I won't accept my limitations now
For neither have I reached my body's peak
nor let my mind give up on why and how

Instead I strive and sweat to keep my vow
With muscles trembling, mind and stomach weak
I won't accept my limitations now

Some others watch me strain and raise their brow
but neither will I heed them when they speak
nor let my mind give up on why and how

They preach of peace that limits can allow
but sill my pace their murmur cannot break
and why accept my limitations now?

So let them set their expectations low
and find their joy without the strength to seek
and let their minds let go of why and how

Achievement is the only peace I know
I spit away the mantra of the weak
I won't accept my limitations now
nor let my mind give up on why and how

WALKING WITH ORION
Catherine Bishop - 2005

I walk at night the quiet fields of home
And let the sky's dark peace empower me
To meet the coming day with mind as free
And tranquil as the lights in heaven's dome.
Familiar stars I greet like favored friends.
I've seen their faces countless times before,
And just as they were named in ancient lore,
They'll swing across the zenith 'til life ends.
Orion stands aloft with shoulders wide
And listens as I tell him of my cares.
From him I borrow strength enough to dare
Tomorrow's trials from dawn to eventide.

His unseen arm across my shoulder lies,
A comfort and a blessing from the skies.

II. ELEANOR HAYDEN

There will be a day when I shall know that I am free;
There will be one perfect step, and I shall walk!
But so gradually strength comes back to me
I shall not note the day, nor feel the step.

Born in 1919 in Mokena, Illinois, a small farming town west of Chicago, Eleanor found her own authentic and unique way of moving through the world from an early age. Her father James Victor Hall taught Eleanor, an only child with few playmates, how to manage livestock, work the crops and shoot a .22 rifle. Her mother Martha Lockwood Hall was an independent and outspoken woman, formally schooled only through third grade, but self-educated in many fields. The Great Depression hit when Eleanor was 10 years old, devastating the U.S. economy. Her father died soon afterward, and she and her mother moved off the farm.

Eleanor attended Cornell College in Mount Vernon, Iowa where she was selected for membership in Phi Beta Kappa and earned a B.A. degree and teaching certificate. She also took flying lessons offered for college credit, completing her private pilot's certification in 1941. As more and more young men entered the armed forces during World War II, Eleanor joined the ranks of women filling the civilian jobs left behind. In 1943, she became an air traffic controller, a challenging job she thoroughly enjoyed and which also led to steadfast friendships with her co-workers.

She met Joseph Hayden, a U.S. Navy veteran only a few years her senior, when they were both employed at Bendix Field in South Bend, Indiana. A romance led to marriage in 1946, the birth of a baby girl the next year, and a move to Lexington, Kentucky in 1948. Eleanor suddenly found herself home all day with a toddler, a newborn second daughter, and her 70-year-old mother. The population in Lexington at the time was not overly friendly to "Yankee immigrants," making for an undeniably stressful and challenging season of life, extended by the addition of an unplanned but welcomed son in 1953. Her poetry from this period echoes a deep and painful loneliness.

As her children grew to school age, Eleanor found her place in the community. An excellent organizer and manager, she immersed herself in community activities from Cub Scout den mother to Girl Scout troop leader, worship liturgist at the Lutheran church and secretary for the Lexington Safety Council. She was also a charter member of the Bluegrass Astronomical Society, sponsor for the Lexington Model Rocket Club, and costume chairman of the professional-level Lexington Easter Pageant. These hobbies and responsibilities filled the mostly-contented hours and days of Eleanor's child-raising years.

After her children graduated high school and left home, Eleanor came to deal with her aging mother's dementia as well as the onset of her own difficult hormonal swings and a recurring brain tumor that caused seizures. She poured the resulting anxiety, doubt, depression and loneliness into a series of nearly 250 sonnets. Her body of work from this period seems to tell the story of a spiritual sojourn that ranges from hopeful to heartbreaking and eventually reveals a glimmer of peace and accord with her life's journey.

Her final years included grandchildren, some travel with her husband and continued dedication to her favorite charities. Eleanor died in December of 2010 at the age of 91.

UNTITLED
1956

Who flies so fierce and free, so high
above the hazy clouds that I
can scarcely find him in the sky?

I see him now: a streaking thing,
hung on a black and silver wing:
alone, unfettered, and a king.

I wonder: might he know, or care,
that once I flew the silvered air,
and knew no terror anywhere?

He then was still a child, no doubt,
who then, as I do now, rushed out,
and stood and dreamed and stared about

to find the flyer in the sky.
Oh, could that flyer have been I
who crystallized his need to fly?

And when his time is past, like mine,
Will he stand down and search the fine
grey mist of cloud, as for a sign

From Heav'n to keep him through the night
Of age, fatigue, and failing sight?
Rememb'ring is faint kin to flight!

SONNET 4
1967

The facile rhymes of simpletons, I think
I knew from birth. The sonnet form is not
so swiftly won. No easy instinct guides
this older hand. No masterpiece is wrought
with ease, or swiftly. No one has in youth
The substance of the soul, or subtle style
of word, or discipline of mind. These come
with years and wounds. The grace of God, the while
it heals, enlarges. So I find myself,
though scarred, with arts I did not have when I
was young and smooth and fair and strong and swift.
Youth would not trade its graces for my wealth,
but time will steal them all. Thank God that I
had pain enough to buy the better gift.

SONNET 18
1967

How foolishly serene I was, secure
the while I dwelt in houses built on sand
I thought was rock. And when the earthquake brought
my house about my head, I found no hand
stretched forth to lift me up and bind my wounds.
It seemed not even God would hear my cry.
I knelt there helpless, wounded and alone.
My impulse was to crawl away and die.
But duty's contract was the godly goad
that pricked me to my feet. I dared not die,
nor even show my pain, for there were some
whose lives were hung on mine. And thus the road
to healing was made clear: the while that I
kept home for them, I made myself a home.

SONNET 331
1967

Oh, thank you, God! Now I have had it all!
I asked for what I thought was overmuch;
You gave me all I asked, and poured on more
I had not dared to hope that I might touch.
Without completely understanding why
I know that I may never ask again.
For what I may desire in years to come
I must await your judgment, nor complain
if you withhold, but only bless your name
for all I have received. Oh, thank you, God!
If memory is all I have, and that
itself grows thin, I shall be bound the same
as I am now to sing, "Oh, thank you, God,
that I have had this day," no matter what.

SONNET 54
1967

Age is not measured by the count of years,
but by the way we spend our energies.
The young go dreaming dreams and making plans;
They feed on future possibilities.
Maturity has little time for dreams:
There is too much of doing to be done.
And when at last the doer stops to rest
he finds, too often, that the dreams are gone,
And in their place is but remembering.
This is the mark of age, no matter when
it comes in terms of years: that force of mind
is not directed to some future thing
Nor spent on Now, but yearns for some lost Then
And reaches back for what was left behind.

SONNET 60
1967

I used to think this wedding band I wore
indelibly confirmed my chosen state:
I was your lifetime voluntary slave,
and proud to be, and quite content to wait
direction of your will. But marriage is
much more than this: not purchase, but an act
of mutual faith , a partnership between
two equal minds and souls that interact
and grow at equal rate. And this requires
disclosure from each one, and that he pay
concerned attention to the other's growth
lest he be left behind. When in my hands
I bore this truth to you, you turned away,
preferring quiet. Well, you can't have both!

SONNET 105
1967

Good night, Old Year. God bless you as you die,
For I cannot: you brought me heav'n and hell:
Imperfect heaven glimpsed in minutes, but
a more than ample time in perfect hell:
The early waking from a dream begun;
The slow starvation of my heart's belief;
The penance for a sin I could not name;
The thieving, cold paralysis of grief.
If all of this can die with you, then I
would speed you to your grave. No dawning day
can bring me pain I have not known; no fate
or threat of doom can further terrify;
I still have life, and I have learned; I pray
my wisdom's not too little or too late.

SONNET 133
1968

I have not chosen Him: He, rather, me.
With every passing day I clearer see
the layers of the proof. I am not free
except within His bonds. What is to be
is set by Him, nor ever changed by me,
nor slowed nor speeded. Though impatiently
I peer ahead, His vast eternity
unfolds by His design, and perfectly
Conceived each second of each day
produces what He planned. His absolute,
eternal, timeless wisdom will prevail,
and only fools contest it, doomed to fail.
I should be wiser then and more astute
if I more willingly did walk His way.

SONNET 223
1969

In all this barren world I have not found
but two whose ears will hear me when I cry
And keep my tortured wailings in their hearts
and never flaunt my weakness publicly;
And both of them are male. I cannot tell
my woman's needs: they could not understand.
They'd lift me up and counsel me to stand
and fight. For men all that is very well,
but not for women. In their "weaker" way
they bend, appear to yield, but persevere
and wait their time. Their need is patient faith,
not infused force. This, then, is what I pray.
God, too, is male, and does not seem to hear.
Shall I then turn to Mary? "Peace," he saith.

III. ON NATURE

WEARY WINDS
Eleanor Hayden - 1938

The pines
Reach their hoary tips into the sky
To make a resting place for weary winds
Too tired to fly.

SPRING MORNING
Eleanor Hayden - 1938

Sun splashes on shining bare branches,
about to come alive,
and drips in spangles
onto dew-grayed grass where no one has yet walked--
where none has dared to move, save spiders,
spinning silver nets throughout the night.

LONG'S PEAK TREK
Catherine Bishop – 1996

These are treasures found today:
Knife-edged breeze and snow-melt's spray,
Crunch of boot on gravel trail,
Pika twitching stubby tail,
Scent of sun-washed rock and pine,
Glades of purple columbine,
Marmot basking on a boulder,
Pack strap pulling at my shoulder,
Miles unwinding. Morning. Noon.
Sunset colors. Rise of moon—
Earth accepts my shrugged-off load.
Blissful rest at end of road.

SPRING ECSTASY
Eleanor Hayden - 1938

Spring is whistling and whispering outside.
I sit in this room, neither out nor in.
Spring dances with the wind on the slanted windowpane;
My feet ache to join the dance.
I walk up a windy hill
and the wind folds about me,
clinging to every curve of my body.
My hair, loosed from its pinning,
runs out ahead of me in my shadow-mirror.
The wind pushes me firmly
off the walk, over the grass, soft carpet for soft earth,
and away down to the sun-silence of the wood lot.

CLIFFSIDE AUDITION
Juliet Lockwood – 2007

With yellow leaf of Aspen
carpeting my path,
I huff and hurry up and up
the cliff-side trail
to hear my heartbeat singing
in my ears, with effort.

Here, abruptly, I am
stopped,
instructed by the rising sun and
setting moon
to join, as best I can, their promenade.

For this surprise
audition, I will tune
into the restless rhythm
nature's cadence.

With the River Rogue below my orchestra,
I set my feet to flight.

The ballet turns I give
in front of this full house of
ferns and nettles thrill me.

And the wind's applause belongs
inside my ears with my own heartbeat's songs.

NATURAL BRIDGE HIKE
Catherine Bishop - 2014

First as a little girl of five years or so
I walked with delight on this trail
Tagging along slowly behind my parents
Amazed at the wide open world
Thrilled at the abundance of pretty white pebbles
Free for the taking

Years later at nineteen with a new boyfriend
His long legs taking him ahead of me
To join his friends at the top
Tagging along as fast as I could go
Eager to be introduced to the knowledge
Of ropes, harnesses, hardware, and sheer rock

Today I climb the path again
Toward the bridge of stone that spans sky and time
Rock-climber boyfriend turned to husband
White pebbles still gem the way after sixty years
The trail remembers my feet

IV. CATHERINE BISHOP

DOUBT

Wrong stood boldly, brashly,
Laughing to the sky,
And laughing shouted, "Claim thy merits, Good!"
And she, standing afar,
Whispered, "They are small, small."

Catherine was born in 1949 in Lexington, Kentucky. Her father Joseph Hayden, a World War II veteran, had used his G.I. Bill benefits to purchase a newly built home on Colony Boulevard in Lexington, Kentucky, part of the Chevy Chase neighborhood. Catherine remembers her family's closest neighbors included an orthopedic surgeon, a university professor, a landscaper, a liquor salesman and a school principal.

In the early 1950s and through her years of public school, she found herself surrounded by families much like her own with fathers working full time and mothers who were homemakers. The middle child with an older sister and a younger brother, she never wanted for companionship. As most homes in those days didn't have televisions or air conditioning, Catherine and her sister and brother spent most of their days outside along with many other neighborhood children climbing trees, playing in creeks, and taking part in backyard games of baseball and other sports.

As soon as she was old enough, Catherine and her sister JoEllen joined the local Girl Scout troop which opened the door to many new experiences and opportunities. She recalls her first "day-out" at

26

a campsite in a neighboring county, complete with hiking, gathering wood, building a fire and cooking their own dinner of "pocket stew." As she grew older, her experiences through Girl Scouting multiplied to include overnight camping, backpacking, horseback riding, canoeing and even caving.

After graduating from Henry Clay High School, Catherine studied at Transylvania University. Her continued enjoyment of the outdoors led her to attend a meeting of the National Speleological Society's local grotto where she met future husband Charlie Bishop. The couple married in 1974 and Catherine welcomed her son Steve in 1976 and daughter Juliet three years later in 1979.

Through the majority of the 1980s and 90s, Catherine stayed home to raise her children. During these years, the family often took weekend camping trips to meet up with the group of friends that had formed in part from those 1970s NSS grotto meetings. The group usually camped at the Park Mammoth Resort in Park City, Kentucky, spending their days hiking the ridges and exploring the various caves on and near the property. The exploits of their group which came to be known as the James Cave Project are detailed in Catherine's non-fiction book by the same name.

The move to Woodford County in 1989 brought to fruition something both Catherine and Juliet had longed for, the chance to live with horses "in their back yard." Over the next two decades, many horses including two feisty mares for Juliet to ride and show and a number of mares and geldings entering their retirement years came and went from the farm. Catherine loved and cared for all of them, finding solace from the changing stresses of life and enjoying their companionship as can be heard in her poem "Whistling" written in 1997.

In the late 1990s and through the first 12 years of the 2000s, Catherine found herself caregiving more and more for her aging parents. From their initial move out of their home on Colony Boulevard and into the Wesley Village Retirement Community, Catherine shouldered the majority of the responsibilities not handled by professionals. She also visited them frequently as their social connections outside the family waned. The physical and emotional toll of those years can be heard in her only sonnet "Walking with Orion" written in 2005.

Even before her parents' passing (Eleanor in 2010 and Joe in 2013), Catherine had joined Charlie in what would become one of their favorite pastimes, running 5-K races and competing in Masters and Senior Games track and field. While Charlie ran middle and long distances and competed in pole vault, Catherine started by learning to throw the shotput and discus and eventually adding javelin, high jump, long jump and triple jump to her repertoire.

These days, having weathered neck and shoulder surgery, Catherine still competes from time to time in less strenuous running and field events. She reflects that while she never wrote any poetry about it, participating in Masters and Senior Games provided many adrenaline-fueled and enjoyable moments, to say nothing of the fellowship and friends she and Charlie made along the way.

Now in her 70s, Catherine enjoys spending time relaxing and reflecting more than she ever had the opportunity to during the various, more physically and emotionally demanding seasons of her life. She can often be found on her back porch with a book in her lap and her coffee within reach.

QUILT OF LIFE
1985

I'm going to weave me up a quilt of life
to show all the lovely things:
A baby's laugh, a wedding ring,
the flash of sun on a bluebird's wing.
I'll piece in all my memories and the colors that I see
And every stitch will count a blessing that the Lord has given me.

I'll use the pink of a dawn-filled sky,
the golden warmth of sun,
The silver moon and stars of night
and evening's peace when the day is done.
I'll add gray clouds from summer storms
and the rainbow's gentle blend
And border it with happy smiles from the faces of my friends.

I'll take the green of summer fields and harvest's golden brown,
The red and orange of falling leaves
and white of snowflakes drifting down.
I'll add the warmth of laughter
'round the crimson hearth-fire's glow,
Yes, all these things so dear to me my quilt of life will show.

I'm going to weave me up a quilt of life
to show all the lovely things:
A baby's laugh, a wedding ring,
the flash of sun on a bluebird's wing.
I'll piece in all my memories and the colors that I see
And every stitch will count a blessing that the Lord has given me.

GREEN RIVER
1994

Golden dawn, diamond sky,
Silver river slipping by.
Waves and breezes blend a song,
Current bears my craft along.
My heart is light, contentment full
As silver paddles dip and pull.
Confined by cliffs and arching tree,
Yet river sets my spirit free.
Then campfire's blaze, stars on high,
And silver, silver, slipping by.

WHISTLING
1996

Whistling a note in the last of the light,
  I call my horses in for the night,
    But with eager ear and high-flung head
      They choose to obey the breeze instead.
        With fingers of wind ruffling their manes
          And tails afloat like raveled skeins,
            They flow before me down the hill,
              Run and whirl and twist until
                It seems they invite me to join in their dance
                  And I run with my sisters, blessed by the chance
                  To be flying free, dancing light,
                  With the silver spirits of the night.

REMEMBERING PIPER
2002

I didn't know you when you were a young foal,
chestnut coat gleaming,
ears pricking at the sound of a mockingbird,
ecstatic at your first taste of clover.

I wasn't there when you learned to race,
flying over steeplechase hurdles,
great heart carrying you to victory after victory.

I don't know how many people groomed you,
saddled you, cared for you, loved you,
let you scratch your head on their shoulders.

Aging, daydreaming, still beautiful,
you spent retired years grazing my fields,
carrying me on bareback sunset rides,
sleeping in oak shade beside your friends.

Today I sent your spirit to rise with the mist,
flying where I can't follow,
running where you will never tire.

And up on the ridge, in deep oak shade,
I can almost see a chestnut colt standing,
fetlock deep in clover,
ears pricking at the sound of a mockingbird.

EDGE
1968

Motionless, alone,
With bowed head I stand,
And a new day breaks.

Wild thoughts arise
As past and future meet harshly here
At the edge of time.

Child of mine,
As yet unfelt within my womb,
Sleep on;
Thine is the only peace in the world.

MIRACLE
2021

The faintest tap on my window
Hummingbird has crashed into a false sky
And lies motionless on the deck
My tear rolls…but then a twitch in the pointed beak
It's not dead, but may be dying
Can I save this tiny jewel?
I cradle it in my hand, its non-weight
Far lighter than the deep heaviness in my heart.
I lower it to the grass
Praying for healing in cool maple shade
A nearly invisible throb in the tiny throat
Eye opens but it's still not moving much
Maybe it needs water
I pick it up, hold its bill to the feeder
Nothing…
…then in a magic instant
It explodes off my hand, racing into the sky
My freed heart rises upward beside it
Feather-light and full of joy

ON HAWK'S WINGS
2021

Red-tailed hawk
Beautiful spirit brother
Together, we ride the wind
We slice the sky
We see clear to eternity
As you lift my soul
Toward heaven.

V. ON DESIRE

DAYDREAM
Juliet Lockwood - 1996

Ah, Bittersweet
since the moment's come and gone
Bitter in your absence now, but
Sweet, you'll come again.

PASSION

Eleanor Hayden - 1938

In the cool and naked darkness
I walked cool and naked, too,
never dreaming, in that darkness,
that I might, perchance, meet you,
walking also in that darkness,
cool and naked and alone;
till I came upon you softly
there, and claimed you for my own--
Claimed you in soft-spoken whispers;
Claimed you, as a sort of lark;
Kissed you, loved you there till dawning,
in the warm and naked dark;
With our souls fast growing closer
and our heads fast growing light,
giddy with the love of loving
in that hot and naked night;
Giddy with the love of loving,
Sick with hurt to find you gone,
Screaming with the anguish of it
in the cold and naked dawn.

GODDESS
Juliet Lockwood – 1997

Naked in my sex dress
I lie in a pink velvet eternity
a luscious flower petal girl
wearing an angel chain
a delicate young storm
raining desire

Lovers drink my wild lust
and devour my kisses like candy
exploring me in a delirious worship.

My belly oceans dance
with a ferocious fevered joy
deep within my center
and slowly, sweetly,
the ache takes leave

I squirm drunk on their embrace
By morning
I will throb
poisoned and broken,
but tonight
I lie beneath self
whispering tongue music
screaming poetry
bleeding for them

SOMETIMES LOVER
Juliet Lockwood - 2002

My sometimes lover
I mount your steps today
not knowing what will happen when I knock
Sometimes you're not here
and I must sigh
and just keep walking down the block

And sometimes you are here
but with another
and I must smile and make some small excuse
to find my way back down your steps and
back onto the street

You do, sometimes, amuse me with your tastes

But oh so sweet
are those
Sometimes
when with a smile, you let me in
and small talk turns to kissing and embracing
and I find you in my arms again
like so much clay

Days like today
Your lips are soft to mine
belong to only me again
It's the others' turn to knock
Soon as I finish you, I'll set you free again
Let you and fate decide
Who will it be next time?

For if we cannot play
and share
kindly
as our mothers taught
then I should not
walk up your steps today.

SWEET ENVY
Juliet Lockwood - 2004

I don't know who to envy more
my new friend caramel
my old friend cream
two dreamy sweets
sweeter made
in mixture seemingly richer
each alone, select
but when combined,
Perfect

And I'm wrecked
because I dream
beyond tasting
I dream of
hopping their dish and
laying wasting
joining their measure
for a fix
of scrumptious crime
I'd almost do the time
for the pleasure

But what a shame
to taint them
I have no place in their taste
and blame is bitter ruin

Not to mention jealousy
from my own
partner flavor

We too are savory
complimentary
meant-to-be

And I would never risk
our classy confection
for a brief caramel cream stint

For my own peppery part
I'll stick with mint

VI. JULIET LOCKWOOD

How many years till
children see a spider's web
only in pictures?

Born in Frankfort, Kentucky in 1979, Juliet Lockwood describes her childhood as idyllic. Her father Charles Bishop worked as a civil engineer and her mother stayed home with Juliet and her older brother until they were both well into their teens. In 1989, the family moved from a suburb in Frankfort to a small farm in nearby Versailles, Kentucky.

The summer before her senior year of high school, Juliet successfully auditioned to attend the 1996 Kentucky Governor's School for the Arts in creative writing. The three weeks she spent at the residential summer program seeded a love for her generation's voice and established within her a firm foundation in both the art and the value of giving and receiving literary critique.

Juliet attended Transylvania University in Lexington, Kentucky, and graduated with her B.A. in English in 2001. Just a few months later, on little more than a whim, she moved with her future husband to Virginia Beach, Virginia.

An odd hybrid between a vacation destination and a military town, Virginia Beach quickly revealed itself as an urban sprawl tacked onto a beach boardwalk. Lacking a university, a downtown or any civic

46

interest in arts and culture, Virginia Beach hit Juliet like a slug to the stomach, especially when paired with the transition from college to professional life. Her longing for Lexington and the life she enjoyed before can be heard clearly in the poem she wrote by the same title.

The five years she spent in Virginia Beach felt like the longest in her life to that point. Juliet and Jay married in 2003, holding their wedding in Kentucky in the chapel at her alma mater, Transylvania University. The wedding counted among many trips back to Lexington which were always happy times for Juliet tinged with a sort of desperation, knowing they were glimpses at the life she could no longer call her own.

She found very little to sustain her creative soul until 2004 when she accepted an invitation from a friend to join a newly forming group dubbed The S.O.F.A. Poets. Meeting in the area known as Ghent in neighboring Norfolk, Virginia, S.O.F.A. referred to the Studio of Fine Art. The group exchanged works each week and returned the following week to offer feedback and critique.

For the first time in years, Juliet felt her own creative spark reflected in the people around her. What started as the S.O.F.A. Poets grew to include peer critique on fiction writing as well and eventually became The Muse Writers Center, which at the time of this publication continues to operate as a thriving non-profit educational organization.

Through finding such a community of writers, Juliet's literary voice came back to her, and it was in these years that she penned the works, "Lexington," "When I Bleed," and "No Limits."

In 2006, Juliet moved with her husband to Grants Pass, Oregon to follow his entrepreneurial opportunity there. The small-town atmosphere, historic buildings, and thriving local theater community felt much more like home to her than Virginia Beach ever had. New friends, new community activities and a renewed zeal for the outdoors filled her hours for the first several years, largely quieting her muse, though the majesty of the Rogue River and the BLM trail to Raine Falls did inspire "Cliffside Audition" originally composed in 2007.

In June of 2009, Juliet welcomed her first child, and as is almost universally true, but rarely talked about, modern motherhood turned her life and her identity as she knew it completely inside out. She wouldn't find consistent time or energy to write again for nearly six years.

Very little about motherhood came naturally to Juliet, but for the love of her children, she tackled the new and often uncomfortable role with every bit of her energy, creativity and ingenuity. Her marriage hit a rough patch in the spring of 2012, just as she was finding out she was pregnant with her second son. The angst and anguish of the changes she endured that summer can be heard in her poem "Morphametasis."

Her return to a robust writing life began gradually in 2015. A monthly poetry slam started up in Ashland, Oregon, 45 minutes down I-5, and Juliet brought poems including "Oregon Blackberry" and "On We Go" into the world specifically for the competition.

With her now-school-age children becoming more independent all the time, Juliet continues to celebrate her hard-earned opportunity to prioritize her writing during this season of her life, especially in contrast to a U.S. culture that tells her she should be focusing her energies 110% on family, "lucrative work," keeping an immaculate home, and maintaining an Instagram-worthy bikini body. A devoted and loving mother, Juliet's writer self remains, unequivocally, the older and wiser woman within her, because as she is quick to point out to anyone who may still be confused, she's been a writer MUCH longer than she's been a mother.

DAUGHTER'S DEMAND
2001

Dear Father
soon to be beloved Dad,

As I am yet contained in halves inside of you and Mom
and as desire has maddened you as you have gazed on her

Decide
before you plant me to allow
that I will someday feel and thrill as you do now.

Acknowledge that the spark that you supply
imparts to my new soul, a greater dowry than
the skin and bone
the blood and breath of life alone

For surely you can feel the reflex it contains
the little death that shakes you as it wanes

Accept the deal you make with me
Someday I'll break your heart

Accept!

Or catch me now before I start.

LEXINGTON
2005

I.
My city waits for me – her straying wisp –
who fell in love with her from rooftop views
who held her hand the way she would insist
before she'd let me cross her avenues.

She nursed me with the knowledge of her streets
and nourished with that knowledge I would roam
through red mud, bluegrass, blacktop, till my feet
turned toward the blue glass tower leading home.

Though born of her, I lived inside her still
enwombed in urban flesh that never broke
I cleaved to her as offspring often will
adoring how she thought, the way she spoke.

Her downtown scrapers growing toward the skies
were mother features to my daughter eyes

II.
Summer
sticky heat
such heat
to make me high
on High Street where I found

Common Grounds
always changing hands
changing styles between its
wooden floors and ceiling fans
but always open

50

Coffee anytime
sweetened with blue, pink and white
packets of
people, art and
conversation

a gift from my
mother-no-more
I fell infatuation
and lay with her enraptured
eyes to eyes
she guided my palms
over her brick belly
concrete breasts and sidewalk thighs.
We thrilled each other till
we body wept.

Kept women we were
neither shameless
nor bearing shame
in our immaculate embrace.
Each morning, I covered her face
in footstep kisses.
Each evening I praised her shape
from my rooftop vista.

Dressing to please my tastes,
she pulled the Kentucky Theater from
its waste in the back of her closet
re-stitched its plush red curtained proscenium
dusted and shined its stained-glass ceiling
and put it on again

powdered her downtown cheeks
with painted horses for
weeks as I rode
one to the next in delight.
Bottle-capped, stone-fenced
whirly-gigged, dream-coated

they nickered and gloated
necks arched in
equine pride.

Now thoroughly decked out
she brought me on her arm
to the Beaux Arts Ball
a masquerade in her honor.
The cold damp stone
of the Radisson basement
transformed by her
builders-to-be
the architecture students from
her largest university.
Their painted faces praised her
as rhythm raised us both
to ecstatic pitch
and we tangled our limbs in music
not caring whose was which.

Wholly each other's
till the day my eyes strayed
to someone of my own flesh
and I woke one morning,
body next to his,
to her silence.

III.
Such silence without anger or reproach
not mother's punishment nor lover's spurn
releasing me, resolving but to watch
through leaps and falls the lessons I would learn.

And when through panes of glass she saw me cry
she summoned Loudon House to deck its walls
Its courtyard rock and roll a lullaby
reverberating through the gallery halls.

And with such gifts she eased my zigzag mind
my friend whose love was great enough to slack
her stride from by my side to just behind
so she might help, though never hold me back.

I left her with a loving lady kiss
and now she waits for me – her straying wisp.

WHEN I BLEED
2005

Too many days and still no blood
just thin cold sweat
and visions of a life no longer mine

where dreams I've held so tight
disintegrate
transforming into raw and strong
potential for the yet unborn.

How loathe I am to slow my pace
now plunging toward success
breath held
I looked not to betroth
my hard-earned spoils to a child

Moored in my anxiety
I'll sway in coming days
on growing waves
imagined baby babble
lullabying my unnumbered fears

soft tiny hands that
wipe away misgivings in my mind until I
smile.

So when I finally bleed, I cry a while.

OREGON BLACKBERRY
2015

You know the Georgia Peach
the Florida Orange
and DC Cherry,
but there's a reason you've not heard
of the Oregon Blackberry.

An invasive species here.
They try to kill her
spray her with poison
cut her off at her stem
turn her up by her roots
but still she survives
with many shoots

Thrives even!
Flouts her success in their faces
Blossomed
Thorned
and Scary
There's a reason you've not heard
of the Oregon Blackberry

I have two native sons
whose birth blood spilled
out in this very valley
like crushed berry seeds
Whereas I wisped my way
across from the opposite coast, against
the jet stream's carry
whose strong winds drowned out your hearing about
the Oregon Blackberry

Black, because my talents ripened
without the favor of notoriety
Berry, because my words taste divine
and you can't resist picking me.

Despite it all

Others named and celebrated
while my fruit remains underrated
still my fame, so seemingly fated,
my juices forcing tasters to tarry

Not much longer till word spreads
about the Oregon Blackberry.

FLAILING
2020

Next to the newspaper
wing-sticky from whacking,
your little legs
FLAILING
in my now-tepid dregs

Do I rinse you
DOWN?

N-n-no...no
I sluice slow, so
You come to rest, still soaking
on the edge

I work around you till I
SCOWL
and rip a shred of paper towel for you

Why you?
Why you, alone?
I watch you fan your wings
DRY and...

Well, I don't actually see you
FLY; you're just gone.

Perhaps it was your flailing
I recognized
the gesture
CAUGHT
my flying empathy

ON WE GO
2017

First light, too bright!
Too cold!
We scream.
Welcome to this deeper dream
Warm touches from the one we know
Exhaustion
Sleep
And on we go

Paper cuts, PB and Js
Words that chastise
Words that praise
Insatiable! We stretch to grow
Experience
And on we go

The perfect party
Music favs
Our style, our wit
all garner raves
Want to hold this moment slow.
Loose-slipping seconds
On we go

Our feet
out cut
from
under us
unfair affliction
torturous
Ouch!

Crunch!
Air sucked through teeth
Claw slow
to rise an inch
but on we go

Best news ever!
Life new lit
blue patched sky o'er
hard-won gift
Stitches out
on with the show
Exhale, Last snip, and
On we go

Our most beloved
new-launched in life
cheer their triumphs
mourn their strife

Heartstrings, Hamstrings
Bit sore, but SO…
what?
We're wiser
On we go

We thought our heart
broken before
but no knock harder
than at this door

Our child!
Our fucking EVERYTHING
Bile summoned by
their suffering

Grow sorrow's gills
Breathe tears

The air
sucked through their teeth
Harder to bear!

Perhaps they stay
Perhaps they go
Perhaps our minds create it all

The fire of time
consumes the same
tinder beauty
as kindling pain

Ticks the seconds
Glimpse
Gasp
Know

Relive in rush
And on we go!

STOPPING BY WORDS
2018
inspired by "Stopping by Woods on a Snowy Evening" by Robert Frost

Whose words these are, I think I know
He lies beside Old First Church though
He will not mind me borrowing
his memory of the falling snow.

My patrons, they may think it queer
to pause my mad rush toward new year
to ponder snow and frozen lakes
the darkest evening of the year.

If Frost could give my shoulder shake
to ask if there is some mistake
my cheeks would burn with my full-earned
admonishment, my pride forsook.

The words are lovely, dark and deep
But I have promises to keep
And sons whose eager needs run steep
And years to go before I sleep
And years to go before I sleep

CHOICES
2019

My poetry is my Instagram-worthy bikini body,
my novel starts are my immaculate house,
and my short stories, my lovingly-tended container gardens.

My children are my children
and my words have never come before their needs.

Every woman, every mother, must make choices with her time, and
for my part
my words
my worlds
my creations
will always take precedence.

Were I a male author, I'd need no such maneuvers.
And statistically, I'd be published sooner.

VII. ON SUFFERING & DEATH

THE PEACE THAT PASSETH UNDERSTANDING
Eleanor Hayden - 1938

Death came close and stood,
And I, in terror, drew away.

Death came closer, and laid his finger on my heart.
It was not cold!
I looked at death: was this the end of all existence?
What is in dying worth all living to attain?
There must be something there, some crowning joy.

I fear no more.

THOUGHTS FROM THE OTHER SIDE
Catherine Bishop – 2011

"…And may she rest in peace."
Yes, I'm at peace.
I've known peace through my years,
As peace flowed all around me,
And I with it.
The laughter of small children and old men,
The smell of fresh-turned earth and Easter lilies,
The warmth of family and fireside,
The light of winter dawn and summer stars.
Peaceful, and good, and to be treasured—
Yet only hints and fragments
Of a Whole I glimpsed but dimly,
And now see face to face.

SONNET 66
Eleanor Hayden - 1967

To spend the years that I have left like this,
Appalled, bereft, directionless; to know
With certainty I have no goal ahead;
To walk erect, but only for to show
A placid face to fool whoever looks
Into belief that I am whole; to fill
My endless seconds with contrived demands;
To know that they are meaningless, and still
My only dike against insanity;
To grow, but not to give what I have gained;
To close myself into a stagnant sea
That has no outlet: where could ever be
A Hell more hellish, or a life more drained
Of Heaven's hope than this one laid on me?

KATRINA
Juliet Lockwood - 2005

Look back
difficult as it is
Thousands of
women screaming
Please, we must have water

Trapped by water

Prisoners
some so young
and with child
Cursing, Weakening,
their milk dry.

Too sad, Too hard
and yet, you stare.

Those eyes,
they pierce you
haunt you
CRUSH you

Cry
Give all your money
but it is too late.
Her tiny baby came early
and is already
Dead

BORDER CHILD
Juliet Lockwood - 2018

Deny her existence for now.
Call her a figment of the "liberal media's propaganda," but
she breathes
she cries
she endures
in the silence imposed on her
she grows

Will she see her parents again?
No one knows, or
no one will say
She's told they didn't care or that they passed away
She dies some inside at these lies
Still, she grows

She bears witness to
the toddler's
wails for her mom
the baby's drying lips and
quieter and
quieter
cries

She comes to measure time
by those who come and go
the days it takes for eyes
wide white with fear
to gray and narrow
the growing stretches between
thoughts of her own needing
the number of times girls are dragged

out screaming and brought
back bleeding

How she will emerge I cannot say
To her parents?
To relatives?
To strangers?
BROKEN
no matter which way
But I can tell you this

When she emerges
her voice will be lightning lit
and she'll mean to use it

Her words, I can't presume,
but I can PROMISE you
when she rains them down
they will crash true with
the thunder of all she's
seen and endured

UNDENIABLE!

Few will deserve to withstand her storm.

VIII. ON DIVINITY & TRANSFORMATION

PRAYER
Catherine Bishop - 2005

God of love, embrace me.
God of peace, fill me.
God of joy, inspire me.
God of forgiveness, cleanse me.
God of knowledge, teach me.
God of mission, send me.
God of strength, hold my hand.

A PSALM FOR SNOW
Catherine Bishop - 2010

Lord, as your uncounted blessings fall on us every day,
So the falling snow has sifted a crystal blanket over the earth,
Pink in dawn light and glowing blue under starshine, a feast for
our eyes.

Thank you for the sound of snow, crunching under my feet,
And for the taste of snow and smell of wet mittens, bringing back
my childhood.
Thank you, Father, for the feel of an icy wind on my face
And the blessing of your warm spirit in my heart.

OVERFLOW
Eleanor Hayden - 1942

Oh, God, Dear God, thank God
My well is not gone wholly dry.
And if for long enough I let
The water seep between the rocks,
From time to time my cup will fill
And overflow, and I can drink again

MEDITATION BRIDGE
Juliet Lockwood - 2020

I bid my mind be still and start to breathe
I ask each active thought to make its peace
until I feel all apprehension leave

Our consciousness can easily deceive
And thus, in search of tension's full release,
I bid my mind be still and start to breathe.

I make my mental journey to retrieve
serenity and clarity and pace
until I feel all apprehension leave

Appealing humbly that I may perceive
a wisdom older than all form or space
I bid my mind be still and start to breathe

I pray divinity its wholeness weave
into my soul its sacred masterpiece
until I feel all apprehension leave

Exchanged, my doubt, anxiety and grief
for love and creativity and peace
I bid my mind be still and start to breathe
until I feel all apprehension leave

SONNET 81
Eleanor Hayden - 1967

I learn but slowly, and I pay in pain
For every bit of knowledge that I gain.
I often wonder if a wiser man
Would not abandon such pursuits, and plan
An enterprise that would return him more
For less investment, for my little store
Of wisdom is so often not enough
To feed the needy and to see me through
The winter of my doubting to the spring
Of faith's rebirth. But, weighing everything
I spend against my gain, I find that I
Cannot reverse my course: it is not my
Decision. Neither cost nor gain is mine.
I am possessed of God and His design.

DEUS CUM VITA
Eleanor Hayden - 1956

I drink the bitters with deep gasps.
The salty taste of tears is in my mouth.
I have so much to bear.
My bread upon the waters sinks,
And brings me no return.

I bear me, weary, out toward my task —

But oh, the sun is still alive,
The wind is wild!
And how can I be sad?

SONNET 136
Eleanor Hayden - 1968

How different this summer from my last:
In peaceful certainty I pass my days.
Freed from impatience, I am useful now,
My force not wasted pointing out my ways
For God to walk nor urging Him to speed;
Not only knowing, but accepting, this:
I am a laborer; the masterpiece
Is not my duty to design, but His.
Nor even mine to know: He has no need
Nor obligation to reveal to me
The master plan, nor even how one piece
Contributes to the whole: no buried seed
May ask what it will bear or grow to be;
No more may I. Accepting, I have peace.

MORPHAMETASIS
Juliet Lockwood – 2012

Butterfly in reverse
I've waned from winged wonder
Once so delicate, so desired and
buoyant on my breeze
But those same wings could
not resist
the stronger gales

blown about and
bullied
by the bluster
I had to muster
strength
and temper
pride

find my old cocoon and fold
myself inside
and yes, I cried!
feeling my wings dissolve

Outside the thunder
shook my branch
and rain pelted
my self-spun confessional
Winds wailed
as if the world too
mourned
my necessary recession

Storm receding
I emerged
Wingless
many footed
grounded
green and robust

shaking the dust of my wings
from my new sparkling ripples

These days, I
inch instead of soar
but what is more
when jet streams roar
above my head
I latch on tight with
many legs

No longer blown away
My foundation finally
strong
I inch along

A dazzling piece of fluttering
stained glass no more
and no longer so prone to shatter
Go ahead
Ask me what's the matter?

At last I can say
"Nothing!"

I'm green and
strong and
tough!

and finally, that's enough!